colour me!

cREATE YOUR OWN

kindness

Published by Collins
An imprint of HarperCollins Publishers
Westerhill Road, Bishopbriggs,
Glasgow G64 2QT

www.harpercollins.co.uk

Illustrations © Clare Forrest
Text © Becky Goddard-Hill

978-0-00-843958-3

Printed in China by RR Donnelley APS. Co Ltd.

10 9 8 7 6 5 4 3 2 1

Thanks to Michelle I'Anson, Lauren
Murray, Kevin Robbins, Gordon MacGilp,
Kitty Chivers and all the team at
HarperCollins for championing kindness.
Thank you Clare Forrest for the
magical illustrations.

This book is dedicated to Susan Eileen
Goddard, my lovely, smiley, beautiful
mum whose heart was filled with love
and kindness.

#CYOKindness

CREATE YOUR OWN KINDNESS

Becky Goddard-Hill

illustrated by Clare Forrest

Introduction
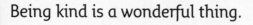

Being kind is a wonderful thing.

The benefits it will bring to you and the world around you are enormous and probably bigger than you could ever realise.

Kindness can achieve so much. For example, it can save species of animals, it can help lonely and homeless people, it can bring families together, it can heal hurt hearts and it can help you be the strongest and most brilliant version of yourself.

Best of all, kindness is a free and beautiful gift that you can give over and over again throughout your whole life.

In fact I would say that, in my opinion, learning how to be kind is the most valuable thing you can learn in life. That's why I urge you to try the activities in this book and to practise being kind until it comes really easily and you're absolutely overflowing with it.

About this book

This book looks at ways to help you create your own kindness with activities such as baking, crafting, journaling and even some martial arts!

With every activity, I share the research or science that is behind it so you understand not just how it works but WHY it works too.

Each topic contains:

- An inspiring quote to motivate you or make you think.

- Science or research that explains how the kindness strategy works.

- An activity to help you put what you have learned into practice.

Being Kind to yourself
Being Kind to others
Being Kind to the world

The activities in this book will help you learn how to be kind in lots of different situations and lots of different ways, even when it might seem tricky.

Each and every scenario will show you how to be the kindness bringer. I think you are going to find it lots of fun.

How you use this book is entirely up to you.

You can dive in and have a go at whichever topic you like, in whatever order you want. Or you can read through the whole thing at once and go back to try the activities when you feel like they might be most useful.

You might want to keep it private, you might want to try things out with a friend or you might want to work through it with an adult. You could even take it in to school and suggest you do one of the activities as a lesson.

It is your book and your kindness journey so the path you take is totally your choice.

Kindness is powerful. Are you ready to give creating your own kindness a go?

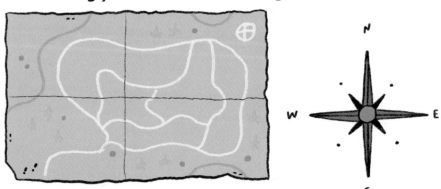

Kindness is about how you treat the people around you, and about how you treat the earth, its citizens, its plants, animals and oceans.

But, while you're busy being kind to everyone and everything else, it can be easy to forget that kindness also applies to how you treat yourself.

Are you kind to yourself?

Many of us seem to find it harder to be kind to ourselves than to other people, but really it is just as important, if not more important, to treat ourselves with kindness.

It's not selfish to treat yourself kindly, it is self-caring and you need to be doing this every single day. When you are kind to yourself, it is easy to spread your kindness far and wide.

Being kind to yourself

1. What is kindness?

Kind people are the best kind of people.
                                        - Unknown

How would you define kindness?

Is it someone giving you their last sweet? Is it forgiving your best friend for being grumpy?

It is, in fact, all of these things and many more. Kindness is about being caring and thoughtful and all sorts of other wonderful words that you can search for in the wordsearch on the next page.

How it works

The word kindness was first written almost 800 years ago and comes from an English word **kindenes** which means noble deeds or courtesy (so doing good things politely).

Kindness can mean different things to different people, but at the most basic level it is always the same. It's about going out of your way to lend a hand, or to bring comfort or joy or healing.

Being kind to ourselves and others is one of the easiest ways to live a happy life.

Activity: Kindness wordsearch

```
U  N  S  E  L  F  I  S  H  N  Z  P  S  C  Z
X  H  U  K  T  E  y  P  H  A  G  M  N  J  R
R  D  G  N  I  R  A  C  V  G  J  E  O  P  M
H  U  Z  N  C  N  T  P  G  N  L  B  I  G  I
J  R  A  F  I  E  D  E  D  U  H  F  T  S  X
Z  F  U  I  E  V  N  N  F  F  H  R  N  J  H
M  N  B  W  J  E  I  T  E  y  C  I  E  E  T
F  N  S  y  R  T  H  G  X  S  Q  E  T  L  y
D  B  I  O  P  G  I  S  J  T  S  N  N  T  y
T  R  U  C  U  W  S  N  S  B  F  D  I  N  U
O  S  N  O  E  V  H  J  y  B  W  L  D  E  T
M  R  H  Q  G  K  I  N  D  X  V  y  O  G  J
R  T  A  Q  I  Q  V  F  Z  B  W  R  O  H  G
B  X  H  E  L  P  F  U  L  N  U  E  G  O  F
Q  G  B  C  B  W  S  Z  I  S  M  R  M  V  Q
```

CARING	GENTLE	KIND	SWEET
FRIENDLY	GIVING	HELPFUL	THOUGHTFUL
GENEROUS	GOOD INTENTIONS	NICE	UNSELFISH

Create your own kindness...

...by thinking about all the things the word kindness means to you.

2. Creating a kindness journal

Three things in human life are important. The first is to be kind. The second is to be kind. And the third is to be kind.

- Henry James (Author)

Energy flows where attention goes, so putting your focus on kindness is a great way to start bringing more of it into your life.

Creating a journal all about kindness will help you to really focus on it. A kindness journal could be a place for you to:

- List some random acts of kindness you might like to try.
- Write inspiring stories that involve kindness.
- Write kind things you have done for other people.
- List the ten kindest people you know.

It is essentially a scrapbook of your thoughts, feelings, ideas and stories about kindness. You can make it as colourful and visual as you like.

Let it be a place to gather your inspirations so you can become even kinder to yourself, to others and to the world.

How it works

Scientists have discovered that the average person has about 60,000 thoughts in a day. That's an awful lot!

When we are creative (in this case writing or doodling in our kindness journals), our minds enter a state of flow. We become totally focused on what we are doing and this lets our busy brains relax, brings down our heart rate and boosts our mood.

Activity: Make your own kindness journal

All you need to make a kindness journal is an unlined notebook and a splash of creativity.

Don't just write! Illustrate, decorate, list make, mind map and use anything and everything that inspires you.

Journals look amazing if you use newspaper cuttings, paint, crayons, coloured pencils, ink, photos, stickers or bits of fabric.

Create your own kindness…

…by creating a kindness journal.

3. Forgiveness

You yourself, as much as anybody in the entire universe, deserve your love and affection.
- Sharon Salzberg (Buddhist meditation teacher)

You are perfect, just as you are.

You are also human, and being human means that sometimes you will get things right and sometimes you will get things wrong.

I bet your teacher is grumpy sometimes, your grandma a bit cross, your sister bad-tempered, your best friend a bit bossy?

And let's be honest, what about you?

You might try really hard to be, but sometimes (because you're tired or fed up, sad or bored or jealous perhaps) you won't always behave that nicely either.

How it works

Researchers have found that criminals who feel some guilt about their bad behaviour, and who feel concern for their victims, are less likely to commit a crime again.

Researchers have also found that criminals who think they are BAD people are more likely to commit more crimes as they think they cannot change.

Criminals who instead see their BEHAVIOUR as bad (rather than themselves) are more likely to feel they can change and behave better going forward.

Concern for the people we have been unkind to is important as it drives us to change our behaviour, but thinking that you are a bad person doesn't help at all.

So no hating yourself, just change your behaviour in future instead!

Activity: Letter of forgiveness

When you do get things wrong, there are some things you need to do to make it better:

1. First of all, apologise.

2. Try and understand why you felt or behaved like that.

3. Figure out a plan for how you can behave better in future.

You have to be kind to yourself (just as you would be to your friend if they'd been grumpy). You have to face it, deal with it, then forgive yourself and let it go.

Write a letter to yourself forgiving yourself for something you regret doing in the space on the opposite page. You need to acknowledge what you did, say how you have tried to put it right, and forgive yourself.

write your
letter here

_____

_____

_____

_____

_____

_____

_____

_____

_____

_____

Create your own kindness...

...by forgiving yourself when you make a mistake
rather than beating yourself up about it.

4. Being your own cheerleader

If you make friends with yourself you will never be alone.
- Maxwell Maltz (Surgeon and psychologist)

Everyone needs someone to cheer them on, to encourage them and to tell them they can do it!

But what if there is no one currently showing you that kindness and being your cheerleader?

When any support is missing in your life there are two things you can do...

1 You can ask someone else for what you need.

2 You can try to help yourself.

How it works

Other people are not mind readers. You may think that X is being unkind because they didn't wish you good luck in your test, for example. But maybe X forgot, didn't realize you were worried, or simply had their mind on other things.

If you asked X to wish you luck and told them you were scared, they most probably would be supportive and encouraging.

Speak up. Sometimes we have to ask for what we need and that's much better than just assuming someone doesn't care.

However...

If the person you have asked to support you STILL doesn't provide you with support, what can you do? Well, you could try asking someone else. But if that still doesn't work then please don't worry. I know someone who is always available to be kind and supportive to you. Go and look in a mirror... there you are! Your very own best friend.

draw
yourself
here

Activity: Talk to the mirror

Try standing in front of a mirror and telling the person you see exactly how wonderful they are. Give them a pep talk if they need encouragement, and wish them well with all the things they are trying to do.

It can feel a bit weird to start with but keep doing this until it becomes second nature.

If looking in the mirror feels a bit uncomfortable, perhaps you could take a photo of yourself or write some little notes of encouragement in the notes on the next page?

Between you and me, I write myself little notes of encouragement in my diary all the time and can often be found talking to myself!

Create your own kindness...

...by being your own best cheerleader.

5. Self-kindness pick and mix

A single sunbeam is enough to drive away many shadows.

- Francis of Assisi (Catholic friar)

Being kind to yourself really does matter, because you matter. Just a tiny act of kindness towards yourself is enough to lift your spirits.

This might feel a bit odd or tricky at first but, if you want to get good at anything in life, you just have to:

1. Make a start
2. Practise
3. Practise
4. Practise some more
5. And finally, practise just that bit more.

The more you try being kind to yourself, the better you will get at it and the easier it will become.

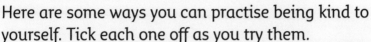
Activity: Practising self-kindness

Here are some ways you can practise being kind to yourself. Tick each one off as you try them.

- [ ] Look at old photos that make you smile.
- [ ] Read a bit of a book you love.
- [ ] Spend time with your favourite people.
- [ ] List five wonderful things about you.
- [ ] Ask someone close to tell you five awesome things about YOU!
- [ ] Finish this sentence: 'I am awesome because...'
- [ ] Learn something new today.
- [ ] Plant an apple seed for your future self.
- [ ] Close your eyes for 5 minutes and go to a place that makes you happy in your mind.
- [ ] Make a playlist of your happiest songs.

If any of these activities make you feel particularly good, you might want to make them a regular part of your life.

Create your own kindness...

...by treating yourself with love, kindness and respect over and over again.

6. Being kind to your body

There is only one corner of the universe you can be certain of improving, and that is your own self.
      - Aldous Huxley (Author)

Being kind and tender towards your body makes a huge difference to how you feel, both physically and mentally.

Below are some ways you can show your body some TLC (tender loving care).

Having a cuddle

Everyone feels better after a cuddle and you can have one whenever you want. Folding your arms over yourself and giving yourself a little squeeze, or gently stroking your arm or your hair are non-obvious ways to give yourself a cuddle.

Physical touch reduces cortisol, the stress hormone in your body. A little bit of self-hugging brings it down and makes you feel much better.

Exercising every day

The World Health Organization says that children aged 5–17 should do at least 60 minutes of physical activity every day. (You don't have to do this all at once.)

Exercising your body helps you feel better mentally, helps you ward off illness, feel stronger, maintain a healthy weight, and have more energy.

Why not try skipping, walking, running, trampolining, ice skating, horse riding, playing football or swimming? Exercising can be great fun. It can also be really sociable if you rope in a friend or family member to do it with you.

Eating well

Imagine if you were responsible for looking after someone else.

Drinking lots of water, eating lots of fruit and veg and having healthy snacks helps your body feel good.

Brushing your teeth

Try seeing your toothbrush as a good friend that helps your teeth look sparkly, your breath smell fresh and your mouth stay healthy. Brushing your teeth well is another tiny daily act of kindness towards your body.

Sleeping well

Sleeping well gives our bodies a chance to rest and revive, ready for the next day.

To get a good night's sleep you could try:

- Going to bed and waking up at the same time every day. This gets your body into a rhythm.

- Having no screen time for an hour before bed.

- Having your own little sleep routine (such as bath, book, bed) and sticking to it.

Your body (and your mind) will work MUCH better if you have a good sleep.

Activity: Create a self-kindness routine

Can you think of other ways to take care of your body and show it some kindness? What could you add to the list?

Come up with some more ideas and add them below to remind you to look after your body.

Create your own kindness...

...by taking good care of your body so it can help you lead the best life it can.

7. Home spa

Caring for your body, mind, and spirit is your greatest and grandest responsibility.
                            - Kristi Ling (Happiness expert)

If you feel in need of a bit of extra self-kindness, pampering your body is a fantastic way to do it.

Warm water can soothe tension in your body and help you feel more relaxed. Put in some lavender-scented bubbles to double the effect. The scent of the lavender can really help reduce tension.

How it works

In a German study, people who were feeling depressed reported a boost in mood after soaking in a bath for 30 minutes. In fact, in this experiment, regular baths proved to be more effective in lifting people's mood than exercise.

Bathing is such an easy way to be kind to your body, it does love a pamper.

Activity: Have a pamper session

Write ideas for your perfect pamper session in the bubbles below.

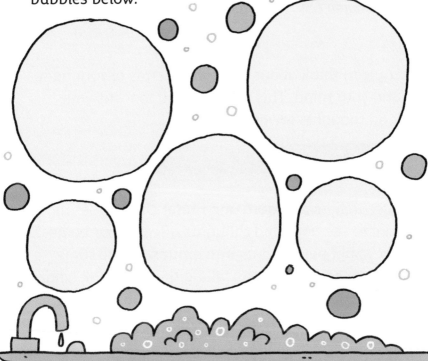

A little bit of pampering can go a long way. Making your body feel well loved and well cared for can be so much fun and being kind to yourself can feel brilliant. Try and make time for it every day.

Create your own kindness...

...by giving your body a little extra pampering every now and again.

8. Thinking kindly about yourself

Wanting to be someone else is a waste of the person you are.

— Marilyn Monroe (Actress)

You can think about yourself in terms of your body and your mind. This can help you to focus your kind thoughts towards yourself.

How it works

Researchers at Oxford and Exeter Universities did a trial to see how kind thoughts affected our bodies. They split participants into groups, where some listened to instructions telling them to think kindly about themselves and the other groups listened to instructions encouraging them to be self-critical.

The group who had been encouraged to think kindly about themselves had a lower heartbeat and reported feeling more relaxed and safe.

The group who listened to the self-critical instructions did not feel so good, their hearts beat faster and they felt threatened and stressed (feeling like this a lot can make you poorly).

Your body

Our bodies are all different, and able to do different things. Being able to see, hear, walk, run, jump, hug – these are all huge privileges that not everyone has. Think about your own body in terms of what it CAN do and you will be amazed. This is more important than focusing on what your body looks like.

It deserves your kindness, your attention and your care, doesn't it? Your amazing, unique body.

What five things do you value most about your body and what it can do?

1

2

3

4

5

Your mind

Your brilliant mind: learning things, helping you make choices, form words, imagine things. Everyone's mind has unique and amazing strengths. Appreciating what your mind enables you to do is a good start to showing yourself kindness.

What five things do you like most about your mind?

What does it do really well?

1 _____

2 _____

3 _____

4 _____

5 _____

Activity: Describe yourself and your best qualities

How would you describe yourself, your talents, personality and abilities in the kindest way possible? Write a list in the space below.

Create your own kindness...

...by really appreciating what your body and mind can do.

9. Being kind to your mind

The time to relax is when you don't have time for it.
          - Sydney J Harris (American journalist)

Do you have a busy, buzzy, chattering mind filled with thoughts flying around at a billion miles an hour?

Sometimes having all that noise in our minds can feel really stressful.

It needs a bit of quiet.

Feeling Zen is when you feel all peaceful and calm. Your mind LOVES to feel Zen. To be kind to your mind, you need to help it feel that way when it all gets too loud in there.

How it works

Tai chi (pronounced: tie-chee) is a Chinese martial art that has been practised for over 800 years. It combines deep breathing with flowing movements.

When you do tai chi you have to focus your mind completely on your movements, and this focus helps your mind become calm and clear.

Activity: Calm your mind

Repeat this simple tai chi exercise ten times to help you feel more relaxed.

1. Sit down on a chair or stand up tall with your legs slightly apart.

2. Rub your hands together quickly as if you were trying to get warm on a chilly day.

3. When they feel warm, stop rubbing but keep your palms touching each other.

4. Now very slowly pull them apart, to about your shoulders' width and breathe in as you do this.

5. Bring them back together as you breathe out, but don't let them touch, and then slowly pull them apart again as you breathe in.

Some people believe this creates a ball of energy between your hands, some say it helps you focus your breath so you become calm and relaxed.

What does it do for you?

Create your own kindness...

...by making an effort to be kind to your mind.

35

10. Speaking kindly to yourself

Talk to yourself like you would talk to someone you love.
                    - Brené Brown (Professor and author)

Words are powerful.

Everyone loves to hear a thank you, a compliment or a word of encouragement. I suggest you shower these sorts of words like sprinkles on a cupcake, at all times. They are such an easy way to bring happiness. Anyone and everyone blooms with a kind word.

Let's think about that for a minute.

If kind words are so powerful then why do you sometimes say horrible things to or about yourself? The way you speak to yourself can have a big impact on how you feel. So you can either encourage yourself or put yourself down with words. It's your choice.

How you talk to yourself matters just as much, if not more, than how you talk to other people.

How it works

A psychologist called Ethan Kross from the University of Michigan performed a series of experiments to see how self-talk affects our behaviour. He discovered that when we use our name when talking to ourselves (instead of saying 'I'), we tend to speak to ourselves more kindly.

Here is an example of my self-talk when referring to myself as I:

'Aaggh, I will never get my book finished.'

But if I refer to myself as Becky, I might say:

'Come on Becky you can do this, time to get writing.'

Try it! Speak to yourself with the sort of words you would use to a friend; cheer yourself on, value yourself, respect yourself, say kind and encouraging words to yourself, forgive yourself.

You are amazing!

Activity: Words of kindness

Speak kindly to yourself by filling in the spaces on the opposite page.

Before you go to bed each night, look at your list and say your answers out loud to yourself. Do this every night for a week.

Remember to use your own name as you say these things to yourself.

(It may sound completely weird to speak kindly to yourself, so if it's too hard for you to say the things out loud, try writing them on the next page instead.)

Once you get used to this kind self-speak, you'll find it becomes easier and actually a really valuable and lovely way to talk to yourself before you go to sleep.

You will feel more confident, have more self-belief and you will feel happier.

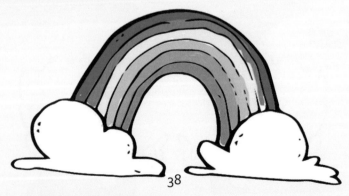

- Thank yourself for something you have done well...

- Encourage yourself with something you are worried about...

- Appreciate something about yourself...

Create your own kindness...

...by speaking to yourself with the same kindness you use when talking to a friend.

11. Creating a comfort box

To be kind to others you must first be kind to yourself.
- Unknown

Sometimes you might feel sad or worried, a bit down in the dumps and upset.

When you feel like that it often really helps if someone can comfort you, listen to your worries, give you a hug perhaps, and help you feel better.

But sometimes no one is around to give you the TLC you need. At those times, you have to give to yourself.

How it works

Researchers in the UK discovered that when we are kind to ourselves it can actually slow down our heart rates, so not only do we feel better in our minds, but our bodies feel more relaxed too. It can also switch off the body's threat response, (its fight-or-flight mode) so we feel far less stressed or anxious.

comfort box

Activity: Create an emotional first aid box

A first aid box contains everything you need for when you hurt yourself.

Let's create a similar box to help you feel emotionally better – a kind of first aid box for your feelings. The things you put inside this box will be there to comfort you if you feel sad.

You might want to make an actual comfort box or choose to create a list of the things you'd put in it. The important bit is knowing what will help if you need to be kind to yourself and knowing that you have those things nearby to help you to feel better.

In my box I would include my favourite book, a soft snuggly jumper I have that feels like a hug, and I'd also put in my guitar.

What would go in your box?

Create your own kindness...

...by reaching into your comfort box when you are feeling blue.

12. Kindness acrostic

Kindness is the quality of being gentle, caring, and helpful.

- Collins English Dictionary

So you know how a dictionary defines kindness, but how do YOU define it?

What meaning does the word kindness have for you? It's important to think about this so it stops being just a word and becomes something you know how to put into action.

A really great way to explore words is to make an *acrostic* poem. An acrostic poem is a poem where certain letters from each line spell out a word or phrase. It doesn't have to rhyme, and it really makes you think about a word and what it means to you.

Activity: Write your own acrostic poem

Try to write your own acrostic poem below. Colour it in when you're done.

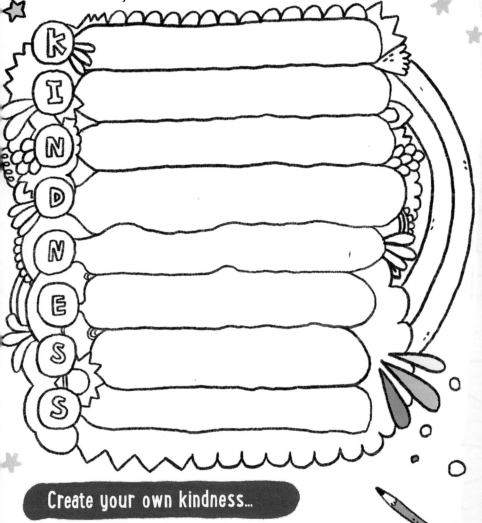

Create your own kindness...

...by really thinking about what kindness means.

13. How to help your kindness grow

Always be a little kinder than necessary.
        - JM Barrie (Author of *Peter Pan*)

We all want to think of ourselves as kind. But that doesn't mean that we don't struggle with it sometimes. Let's have a think about the thoughts that can get in the way of kindness.

shyness

Jealousy

FEAR

not knowing what to do

unkind thoughts

embarrassment

ANGER

WANTING TO BE POPULAR

Can you think of a time when you could have been kind but something stopped you?

The good news is you can become kinder with just a little bit of effort and attention to how you behave and who you hang out with.

How it works

We are not fixed and set in who and how we are.

Our brains grow and change all the time – this is called neuroplasticity. The more we do something, the more our brains develop and strengthen around that behaviour. When we are young it is especially easy to change the way we think as we are not too set in our ways. So being kind can be learned, just like any other behaviour, by being practised again and again.

We also learn things by copying people.

Mirror neurons are cells in the brain that help us imitate other people, and they're especially active during childhood. So much is learned from observing other people and our brains take this in and build neural pathways that help us copy the behaviour.

Spend your time with kind people and watch closely how they behave.

(If you don't know any kind people to hang out with, try reading about kind people or watching movies about kind people to see how they act.)

Activity: Find your kindness role models

Make a list of kind people you know (try to think of teachers, coaches, relatives, friends, anyone at all!). Once you have your list, make a special effort to spend more time around these people.

write you
list here

Movies about kindness

- *Up!*
- *Wonder*
- *Inside Out*
- *E.T. the Extra-Terrestrial*
- *The BFG*
- *Pay it Forward*
- *Homeward Bound: The Incredible Journey*

Books about kindness

- *Jemima Small versus the Universe*
- *The Boy at the Back of the Class*
- *How to Train Your Dragon*
- *The Lion, the Witch and the Wardrobe*
- *Winnie-the-Pooh*
- *Charlotte's Web*

The world around us, the people in it, what we watch and what we read have a huge impact on us. Deliberately make your influences as kind as possible and watch your own kindness bloom.

Create your own kindness...

...by surrounding yourself with it!

14. The kindness cake

Why do we put candles on the top of birthday cakes?
Because it's too hard to put them on the bottom!

I love a good cake, don't you?

What's your favourite kind of cake?

Did you know...?

The world record for eating cupcakes is 72 in 6 minutes. It was set by a man called Patrick Bertoletti in 2012 (definitely don't try this at home).

And

An old English superstition says that if you put a piece of fruit cake under your pillow, you will dream about the person you are going to marry (and make a huge mess).

My kindness cake

I like lemon drizzle cake, chocolate cake, butterscotch cake, Victoria sponge cake, ginger cake, coffee cake, red velvet cupcakes, butterfly cakes and, oh, I really could go on.

Isn't it amazing that such a mix of different ingredients can come together to make a cake?

Quite astonishing.

If you think of kindness as a cake then lots of things go into creating it, don't they? Could you come up with a recipe for kindness cake? What would these ingredients be and what would the end result look like?

Ingredients for my kindness cake
100g of caring
2 spoons of thoughtfulness
500g of patience
And for the topping I would have a dollop of kind words

Activity: Create your own kindness cake

What five ingredients would go into your kindness cake?

And what would you use for the topping?

Ingredients

1

2

3

4

5

And for the topping

1

2

3

Directions

Mix well and be proud of what you make from your ingredients. Have a big slice yourself, and then share it with everyone you meet!

What would your cake look like?

Your cake will need a name too.

Create your own kindness...

...by baking it into a cake.

15. The cup of kindness

You can't pour from an empty cup. Take care of yourself first.

\- Unknown

I'm going to ask you to do something rather strange and think of yourself as a cup.

When you are full to the brim of happy thoughts and loving feelings, it is easy to pour from your cup and for you to spread your joy and treat others with kindness.

Sometimes though, our cups aren't full and we may feel a bit rubbish. It's not very easy to be nice to other people when you are feeling a bit down and your cup is empty, is it?

You could sit around and wait for other people or the world to be really nice to you before you feel okay again, or you could take charge and fill your own cup.

Knowing how to fill up your own cup when it is empty is really important. People call this self-care or self-love. I like to call it 'self-cup filling', which is much snappier.

How it works

There are so many benefits to being kind to ourselves that can be backed up by science again and again. One of my favourite ways to be kind to myself is to have a really good giggle.

Scientists have found that when we laugh, cortisol (the stress hormone in our bodies) decreases, and dopamine and serotonin (which bring about joy) increase.

So switching on that funny TV show or listening to some jokes is one way to fill you up with the good stuff.

Activity: Fill your cup with kindness

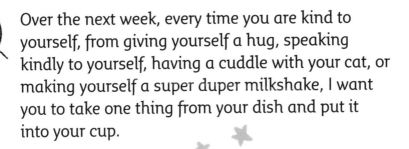

You will need:

- A cup.
- Lots of small pieces of either pasta, buttons, pompoms or pebbles which you should place in a dish next to your cup.

Over the next week, every time you are kind to yourself, from giving yourself a hug, speaking kindly to yourself, having a cuddle with your cat, or making yourself a super duper milkshake, I want you to take one thing from your dish and put it into your cup.

Your aim by the end of the week is for your cup to be FULL. This will represent all the kindness you have shown to yourself.

My belief is that if you have filled your cup even part way up with kindness towards yourself you have probably found it much easier to be kind to other people this week too.

Create your own kindness...

...by keeping your own cup full.

16. Valuing yourself

You're always with yourself, so you might as well enjoy the company.
                    - Diane Von Furstenberg (Designer)

Valuing yourself is important; it protects you from other people putting you down, fills you with confidence and helps you speak kindly to yourself.

An inner critic is an unhelpful voice in your head that tells you you're rubbish or mean or lazy or ugly.

How it works

Psychologist Leon Seltzer says a really great way to deal with the inner critic is to find evidence that proves it wrong.

If it tells you you are lazy, respond by recalling the time you helped paint a garden wall for 5 hours! Or if it tells you you have always been rubbish at maths, tell your critic your last test was better than the one before and you are improving and learning all the time.

Valuing yourself can feel tricky (at first) but I want you to throw yourself into it. Keep it entirely private if you like but I want you to BIG YOURSELF UP!

Write your name in the centre of this page and fill the space around it with words to describe what amazing things make you YOU.

ite your
name here

Create your own kindness...

...by appreciating how special you truly are.

When we are kind to others not only do we make them feel happier, we also make ourselves feel happier.

When I was 8 years old I went on a brownie pack holiday. We went for a long walk and got a little bit lost.

One little girl, quite a bit younger than me and tiny, started to cry. She was homesick, tired, cold and wet so I gave her a piggyback and sang songs to her all the way back to camp to lift her spirits.

I'd been feeling a bit rubbish myself, being lost in the rain is not fun. Singing to this little girl and cheering her up cheered me up too.

When you give, you always receive something back. Making someone else feel better makes you feel better.

Kindness is cool and you never ever lose out when you put your energy into being kind to someone else.

Being kind to others

17. Superstar siblings

Your siblings are the only people in the world who know what it's like to have been brought up the way you were.

- Betsy Cohen (American businesswoman)

Although you might just take your brother or sister for granted, they are actually an incredibly important part of your life.

How it works

Research has found that by the time you are 11, you will have spent more time with your sibling than with anyone else at all including your parents and yourself! It is going to be one of the longest relationships you have in your life so do take care of it and make it a good one.

Scientists also suggest that another person is much more likely to be kind themselves if they see you being kind.

So, it follows that if you are kind to your sibling, they are likely to be kind to you and as a bonus you will feel full of energy.

Activity: Be a kind sibling

Showing interest, sharing special times and giving respect to your siblings will really help you feel much closer. Over the next week, try and do one of the things on each of the lists below each day. Tick them off as you do them.

Ask questions to show you are interested

- [ ] How was their day?
- [ ] Who did they play with today?
- [ ] What are they reading?

Share special times with them

- [ ] Watch a movie together.
- [ ] Look at old photos together.
- [ ] Give them a lovely, sincere compliment.

Respect them

- [ ] Always ask before borrowing their stuff.
- [ ] Accept that you are different and they won't always want to do the same things you do.
- [ ] Don't tease them endlessly.

Create your own kindness...

...by being an amazing sibling and showing them how it's done!

18. Getting to know your grandparents

Grandparents aren't old, they've just been having fun longer.

— Unknown

If you are lucky enough to have kind and loving, fun and caring grandparents then you really have something very precious in your life.

We sometimes don't give our grandparents the care and attention they deserve. We wouldn't expect our friends to buy us gifts, check how we are, turn up at our school shows and sporting events, and always cheer us on without doing nice things back.

Yet somehow and sometimes, with grandparents the giving back gets forgotten and the relationship can be a bit one-sided, with them doing all the work.

Did you know...?

- The UK has approximately 14 million grandparents.

- Grandparent's day is celebrated on the first Sunday in October in the UK. It started in America and has now spread worldwide.

- The average grandparent has four grandchildren.

Whether you see them every day or just once or twice a year, you can be pretty certain your grandparents think about you an awful lot.

You are their child's child and that makes you very special.

Your grandparents may show you kindness in lots of different ways – sweets, letters, cookies, gifts, playing with you, telling you stories, helping you out, giving you hugs.

Share regular photos and news through a family sharing app

Grandparents love to hear what you have been up to, so sending them little updates and sharing photos is a great thing to do.

Play games they enjoy

Find out what games your grandparents enjoy instead of always getting them to play your favourites. They might introduce you to some brilliant card games or show you how to play dominoes or shut the box!

Invite them along

Being old can be pretty lonely sometimes and being invited for dinner, to a show you are in or just to go for a day out shows your grandparents you love to spend time with them.

Ask to see their photo album

One great advantage of living a long time is that you have many people in your life and stories to tell. Your grandparents will love showing you their photo albums and you will learn so much about your family history.

Activity: The grandparent interview

Really getting to know your grandparents and showing an interest in them is the ultimate kindness. Here are some questions you could ask:

- What was your nickname when you were young?
- What is your favourite childhood memory?
- What was the name of your school?
- Who did you play with?
- Did you have any pets?
- Were you scared of anything?
- What was your favourite playground game?
- What did your parents do for a job?
- What were your grandparents like?
- What music did you listen to when you were young?
- Where did you go on holiday when you were young?
- Can you remember your first job?
- Can you remember your first date?
- What's your happiest memory?
- What do you like most about being my grandparent?

Create your own kindness...

...by showering your grandparents with the same care and attention they give you.

19. Fabulous friends

What you do not want done to yourself, do not do to others.

- Confucius (Chinese philosopher)

Are you a good friend?

Do you check in on your friend who is off school?

Do you wish them good luck in their netball match?

Do you notice when they are a little quieter than normal?

Being a good friend means looking out for your friends during the good times and the bad.

How it works

Studies have shown good friends can help us live longer and feel less stressed. They can even make our brains bigger (yes, really!).

It is well worth making an effort to have good friends.

In your diary or on a piece of paper, divide a page into two columns. In one column write down how a good friend treats you and in the other column write down ten things a not-so-good friend might do. It should look something like this...

Good friend	Not-so-good friend
Listens	Teases me
Makes me laugh	Puts me down
Includes me	Leaves me out

Now I want you to take a look at all the qualities you have put in the good friend list and really think about whether you do those things yourself.

It's all very well thinking about how you want people to treat you but what you need to focus on MORE is how you treat them.

People tend to treat you well if you treat them well – the better the friend you are, the better friendships you will have.

Create your own kindness...

...by being the kind of friend you would want to have.

20. Awesome empathy

Wherever there is a human being there is opportunity for kindness.

> - Seneca (Roman philosopher)

Empathy (pronounced: em-path-ee) means imagining or sensing what someone else is thinking or feeling. Trying to put ourselves in someone else's shoes helps us to really see and hear what is happening for them and that makes us kinder in our reactions towards them.

Let me give you some examples of how empathy works.

Your friend is sad because her mum is ill. You want to help so you might think of throwing her a surprise party to cheer her up.

But if you really watch her and listen to her you may sense she is worried as well as sad and that she is in no mood for a party. Your empathy will tell you that a greater kindness would be to give her a chance to talk over her worries, so perhaps inviting her for tea and listening to her would be kinder?

You are part of a group teasing a friend about getting zero on the spelling test. Everyone is laughing, even your friend. But look closer, their smile probably doesn't reach their eyes and actually their cheeks are red and they look embarrassed.

Rather than just carry on you could show your empathy by changing the conversation or distracting everyone with a new game. You could also give your friend a quick hug and check in on how they are feeling.

You don't have to be a mind reader. You can ask people how they are doing and when they have finished talking you can ask how you can help.

How it works

Neuroscientists (brain scientists) at the University of California have found that a special group of brain cells called mirror neurons are responsible for us feeling what others feel. These cells enable everyone to mirror feelings such as pain and joy and sadness. Even babies have them – if one baby cries, it often sets off all the other babies in the room.

How to increase your empathy

It's fairly easy to show empathy and be kind to people in your circle but what about people outside your circle?

It might seem harder to understand people of different races, nationalities, ages and abilities, or simply people you don't know. But you can work on this by paying attention to them.

Are you ever told to stop, look and listen when it comes to crossing the road? Well, that's exactly what you need to do when it comes to showing empathy.

 Stop – Stop thinking about yourself and really pay attention to the other person.

Look – Observe what's happening and think about how you can help. Do you see a child playing by themselves every break time? Try to imagine how this might feel.

Listen – Try and hear what people have to say, especially when they are talking about their feelings. Don't rush straight in with things you want to talk about.

Can you make a 'stop, look and listen' bookmark and keep it in your reading book so you are constantly reminded to do this? Design it in the space below.

Create your own kindness...

...by showing empathy towards other people and learning to stop, look and really listen to them.

21. Before you speak, THINK

When words are both true and kind, they can change the world.
- Buddha (Spiritual teacher and religious leader)

Before you speak:

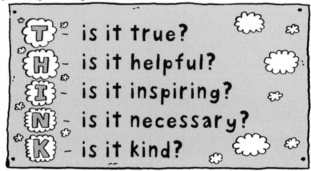

- T - is it true?
- H - is it helpful?
- I - is it inspiring?
- N - is it necessary?
- K - is it kind?

Here's an example of the difference it makes:

Your little sister does a rubbish cartwheel and asks you, 'Did you like my cartwheel?'. Before you say, 'Oh it was absolutely rubbish', you might want to think first.

If you say it was rubbish, how is she going to feel?

You don't need to lie and say her cartwheel was the best you have ever seen in your life or anything like that. But how about telling her it was a great attempt and would she like you to help her practise some more?

How it works

You may think that you can't help the words that blurt out of your mouth because thinking and speaking happen so fast. However, language researchers have discovered that we do plan our speech in different ways and we do have time to think before talking even if it's only a tiny little bit.

If you are really struggling to find the right words then take yourself away for a bit so you can try to think things through, especially if you are in a bad mood or feeling cross. And if you get it wrong and say something unkind and hurtful, apologize quickly and sincerely – that can help a lot.

Activity: Make a poster

Can you make a colourful THINK poster to hang in your classroom or on your fridge? The more people that remember to be kind when they speak, the happier everyone will be.

Create your own kindness...

...by speaking words of kindness and encouragement.

22. What to do about bullying

If there are no heroes to save you, then you be the hero.
                                              - Unknown

People can be bullied for their race, sexual orientation, size, religious beliefs, a disability, their looks or for no obvious reason at all.

It always hurts people inside even if they don't show it on the surface.

If you are a bully

Nobody wants to think they're a bully, but if you find you are intentionally leaving people out, pushing them around, hurting them or spreading nasty rumours about them, then you are in fact bullying them.

Lots of people have displayed bullying behaviour in some shape or form in their lives, but it can hurt others badly and affect them long into their future both physically and mentally.

If you are finding it hard to stop bullying, confide in a grown-up you trust and ask them to help you work out a way to stop this.

Witnessing bullying

If you witness bullying and aren't sure what to do it can be confusing and upsetting.

You have to think, though, is it kind to do nothing?

Sadly, if you do nothing the problem will continue. If you are able, it is better to do something to help.

Talk to an adult you trust and ask them to help you. A teacher is often a good place to start if this is happening at school.

Racial bullying

Racial bullying is where someone's bullying focuses on a person's race or culture. They might be called racist names, be treated differently because of their colour or made to feel like they have to change how they look.

It is not enough just to not be racist, you need to be ANTI-racist. This means taking action against racism. You can do this by supporting friends who experience racism and by trying to imagine how they might feel. You can also report racism to an adult whenever you witness it.

If you are being bullied

IT IS NOT YOUR FAULT. No one deserves to be bullied. Ever. **That is a fact.**

Lots of people get bullied and many adults say it's part of growing up. But it should not be and the biggest kindness you can do for yourself is to take action to make it stop.

You can try telling the person doing the bullying how you feel and ask them to stop behaving that way. They may think they are just playfully teasing and not realise how much it is hurting you.

If this doesn't work or you are too scared, then walk away and tell a grown-up you trust.

No one at all has the right to make your life miserable. You are not powerless. You have a voice so keep talking until someone hears you.

If it's happening online it is just as serious as if it's happening in person so do get help.

Activity: Speak up with silence!

It can take courage and strength to ask for help, but sometimes people don't know you are suffering unless you tell them. Getting help is the ultimate kindness to yourself.

Statistics show that over 50 per cent of people who are bullied never tell anyone. Could you raise money for an anti-bullying charity by having an hour or two's silence and getting sponsored?

Not only would it support a great cause, it would also encourage everyone who takes part to think about their behaviour in relation to bullying.

dON'T KEEP QUiET ABOUT BULLyiNG!

Create your own kindness...

...by speaking up about bullying.

23. Bringing kindness home

You cannot get through a single day without having an impact on the world around you. What you do makes a difference, and you have to decide what kind of difference you want to make.

- Jane Goodall (Primatologist)

There are so many wonderfully different types of family. But there is one thing that makes them all the same...

Families thrive on kindness.

How it works

A 2015 study in the *Journal of Applied Psychology* demonstrated that making sarcastic comments and exhibiting rude behaviour spreads. You definitely don't want that in your family home, so don't do it if you don't want your family doing it!

The good news is that kindness also spreads. In one experiment at the University of Cambridge, viewers were shown either a nature documentary, a funny clip or an uplifting talk. Afterwards they were asked to volunteer to help with a task. People who watched the inspiring talk were much more likely to help.

Researchers believe this is because when we see someone be kind to another person, it gives us a good feeling, which causes us to go and do something kind ourselves.

So if you are kind within your home, there is a very good chance your family will be kinder too and your home will become a happier place to be.

It is possible to show your family how much you care through tiny actions that take very little effort but make a big impact:

- You could do a chore for your sister.
- You could offer to load the dishwasher when it's not your turn.
- You could share a funny story at dinner.
- You could offer to help make dinner.

Being helpful might suddenly seem like a lot of work but just one tiny thing every day doesn't take up much time and really will make your family smile.

Whole family kindness activities

You could take a lead in suggesting kindness activities for your whole family to do.

 You could suggest family activities like feeding the ducks, making a wildflower garden, or perhaps painting an elderly neighbour's fence (with their consent!).

This way you are modelling kindness to the rest of your family and you get to spend some fantastic quality time together.

Activity: Kindness diary

Over the next week, try and fill in the chart on the opposite page with something kind you have done with or for your family. You can make this a secret project or you can stick it to the fridge and show everyone what you're up to. Maybe they will want to join in and fill their acts of kindness in too?

My FAMILY KINDNESS DIARY

WEEKDAY	ACT OF KINDNESS
MONDAY	
TUESDAY	
WEDNESDAY	
THURSDAY	
FRIDAY	
SATURDAY	
SUNDAY	

Create your own kindness...

...by putting it at the heart of your home.

24. Everybody needs good neighbours

In order to have good neighbours, we must also be good neighbours.
- Harry S Truman (Politician)

Very often people are so busy and so caught up in their own lives that they have no idea who is living next door to them.

Neighbours can be amazing. They can keep an eye on your house when you go on holiday, take in parcels if your family is out, be interesting to talk to and fun to spend time with.

Did you know…?

A 2019 study showed that one in three people in the UK don't even know what their neighbours look like. And that over a million older people say they go more than a month without speaking to a friend, neighbour or family member.

Yet the good news is that in a study of 2,000 people, over 66 per cent said that talking to a neighbour made them feel happier.

So it is definitely worth making the effort to be a good neighbour.

Activity: Be more neighbourly

Take a look at this list of ideas for ways in which you could be a better neighbour.

- Smile and say hello when you see them.
- Your family could let them have their phone number in case they have an emergency.
- Take them a few cookies when you bake.
- Try (hard) to stop your ball from going in their garden.
- Wheel their bin back for them after it has been emptied.
- Sweep the leaves from in front of their house.
- Send them a Christmas card.
- Offer to help shovel snow.
- Offer to do chores for older or poorly neighbours.

Do bear in mind that some people are really private and like to be left alone, so please don't worry if your neighbours don't want to be neighbourly – at least you tried!

Create your own kindness...

...by being a good neighbour.

25. Gift giving

The greatest gifts are not wrapped in paper but in love.
                                                    - Unknown

Gifts almost always make people happy. It's not just the actual gift though is it? It is the fact that somebody has thought about you, wants to treat you, and has taken the time to wrap your present because they want you to be happy. All that is just as lovely, if not even more lovely, than the actual gift.

Gift giving is a brilliant way to show someone how much they mean to you.

who   do   you   want   to
    GIVE GIFTS   to?

How it works

Researchers at the National Institutes of Health measured brain activity among individuals who both gave and received gifts. In both cases, the parts of the brain associated with reward were really active. When these bits of the brain are active, we work hard to keep them that way so we are more likely to behave that way again.

Once you start giving gifts and get that buzz it is hard to stop! And it feels JUST as good to give a gift as to receive.

whAt do they like?

Here are some ideas for home-made gifts you might like to try:

- A DIY hot chocolate kit.
- A bunch of flowers from your garden.
- Homemade fudge.
- A bath bomb.
- A drawing of their pet.
- A playlist of songs to make them smile.
- An apple seed, some soil and a little plant pot.
- A wordsearch you've made (you could even photocopy the one from this book, I don't mind).

- A gift of a book you have read and loved.
- A stone paperweight you have decorated and varnished.
- Homemade coconut ice.

Who are you going to make a gift for today?

Activity: How to make chocolate jazzies

All you need:
- Chocolate to melt.
- Sprinkles.
- Baking paper.

There is often an abundance of chocolate left over at Easter, birthdays or at Christmas and it is a LOVELY thing to share.

Chocolate Jazzies are so simple to make and taste delicious. They make brilliant gifts.

1. First of all, line a baking tray with baking paper

2. Melt the chocolate in a microwave, checking every 30 seconds to see if it's smooth. The chocolate will be hot so you may need an adult to help with getting it out of the microwave

3. Spoon out little circles of chocolate onto baking paper about the size of 10 pence pieces

4. Next, shake hundreds and thousands all over the top of your chocolate circles. Pop the tray into the fridge to set and an hour or two later your Jazzies are ready.

Create your own kindness...

...by giving a homemade gift to someone special.

26. How to cope with unkindness

I will not let anyone walk through my mind with their dirty feet.
 - Mahatma Ghandi (Lawyer and peace activist)

Life can be confusing can't it sometimes. You might not feel you are being bullied exactly but you might feel like someone is being unkind to you in ways it is hard to explain or pinpoint.

All of us at some time or other experience unkindness (and all of us really dislike it!).

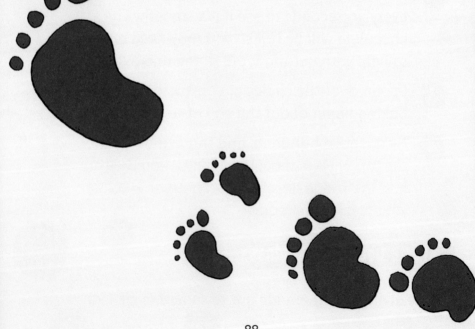

What to do when someone is unkind

If someone is unkind to you it is important to either:

1 Stand up for yourself.
2 Step away from them.
3 Get help to sort it out.

I would advise asking a grown-up for support anyway in helping work out the best thing to do if you are unsure.

Why are people unkind?

Sometimes people are unkind because they are sad, thoughtless, tired, poorly, fed up, hungry or feeling a bit rubbish.

If you usually get on really well and they are usually kind, you may decide to forgive them. Do tell them though (maybe a little later) that you didn't like how they treated you and not to repeat it.

Sometimes though, people are unkind a lot or in a big way and that's really NOT OKAY and that's when you need to take action.

How it works

Research has shown that people who are unkind are unhappy and strike out at other people in their unhappiness.

Studies have also shown that if someone's self-esteem is low, they think that by putting someone else down, their self-esteem will rise.

It is important to understand this so you know their unkindness is about them not about you. But it does not mean, that you have to take it.

How to cope with unkindness

Don't take on board what someone has said in a moment of unkindness. Try not to think about it over and over again. Remember that it's all about what THEY are feeling, not about who YOU are.

Keep your confidence up by reminding yourself of all your wonderful qualities, and spend lots of time with people who really like and appreciate you.

Activity: Practise responding to unkindness

How might you deal with the following situation?

Sarah

Sarah invites the whole class to her party but doesn't invite you. You think it's because you were made captain of the football team instead of her. She's usually okay with you but does get cross when she doesn't win things. What do you do?

1. Shout at Sarah and tell her she's horrible.

2. Turn up at the party anyway.

3. Say horrible things about Sarah to everyone else.

4. Have a quiet word with your teacher, telling them how you feel.

5. Assume everyone hates you and cry for a week.

If you do any of 1-3 it could all go horribly wrong and you could get into trouble. Number 5 just isn't true. So do talk to your teacher or a trusted adult. They may well have a chat to Sarah or her parents and try to sort this out on your behalf.

Create your own kindness...

...by taking action when someone is unkind to you.

27. How to be kind when you don't really like someone

Love and kindness are never wasted. They always make a difference.
— Barbara De Angelis (Author)

Now (and you might feel uncomfortable about this one), let's take a look at those situations where YOU just don't like someone or get on very well with them.

How do you avoid being unkind to them, leaving them out or thinking bad thoughts about them?

Look for the good

You could try really hard to look for something good about them each time you see them. Do they have a nice smile? Are they funny? Are they polite? Are they good at taking turns?

We often find what we look for. If you come into contact with someone expecting not to get on with them, you will often see their faults.

Sometimes we might think that because of someone's age, race, disability or gender we will have nothing in common with them. This is far from the truth...

Diversity (difference) is interesting and fascinating and makes the world a richer place. No one is less than you or more than you. We are all equals and yet everyone is special and interesting in their own way and always worth getting to know.

Keep your eye out for what makes someone fascinating and you will be sure to find it.

How it works

Research at the University of British Columbia found that when people thought about how kind and giving they had been in the past, it made them happy and they were then much more likely to be kind again.

Being kind puts us in a good mood and being in a good mood makes us more kind. It's a wonderful loop! So not only will someone else feel better if you are kind in your thoughts and actions towards them, but you will too and being kind will become even easier as a result.

How to get on better with someone

You could try:

1. Saying hello
2. Smiling
3. Saying 'well done' to them for something
4. Asking them a question such as 'how was your weekend?' or 'did you find that spelling test hard?'

These are all just small gestures that don't take much effort but can really help stop you being uncomfortable around that person and feeling unkindly towards them.

You don't have to be their friend but it's really best not to feel that anyone is your enemy. No one gains from that.

You could make a difference

We cannot know what is going on in someone's life to make them quiet, withdrawn, grumpy or picky – maybe they are having a really bad time at home or they are ill or someone they love is. Being polite and a little bit kinder could make all the difference to their tough time.

Activity: Make your own lava lamp

A lava lamp is a great example of how we don't have to gel together in order to be able to float along side by side in a happy state.

1 Half fill a jar with water (tall thin jars or glasses work best).

2 Add a few drops of food colouring and whisk it around.

3 Carefully pour in vegetable oil until the jar is three-quarters full.

4 Add a spoonful of salt a bit at a time and watch your lava slowly rise.

Oil is lighter than water so it floats on top. Salt is heavier than oil so it sinks down, taking some oil with it, but then once the salt dissolves, back up goes the oil!

We don't have to be alike to get along and we don't have to mix in order to live peacefully together.

Create your own kindness...

...by challenging your own unkind thoughts and living in harmony with everyone.

28. A loving-kindness meditation

A single act of kindness throws out roots in all directions, and the roots spring up and make new trees.

— Amelia Earhart (Aviator)

You may think that in order to be kind you have to take action, but sometimes kindness can be as simple as a wish for the wellbeing of others.

Meditation is the practice of thinking deeply or focusing your mind for a period of time. A loving-kindness meditation is where you focus on sending feelings of kindness and warmth towards other people and then back to yourself. It comes from the Buddhist tradition and is sometimes called *Metta Bhavana*.

How it works

Loving-kindness meditations have been shown to have a HUGE amount of benefits: increased love, joy, contentment, gratitude, pride, hope, interest, amusement and awe. It improves emotional intelligence, helps with illness and relieves stress! It helps you feel connected to others and kinder towards yourself.

Activity: Meditation

Sit comfortably, close your eyes and place your hand on your heart.

Imagine someone you love smiling at you. Take in what they are wearing, how their eyes crinkle and what their smile looks like.

Say to them...

- May you be happy.
- May you be well.
- May you feel peace.

Feel your heart beat nice and steadily and imagine it filling up with warmth and love.

Then keep your hand on your heart and say to yourself...

- May I be happy.
- May I be well.
- May I feel peace.

Create your own kindness...

...by sending out kind thoughts.

29. The power of a simple smile

If you see someone without a smile, give them one of yours.

> \- Unknown

When I was at school there was a sign on the door of my French class that said, 'Everyone smiles in the same language'. I thought, 'Well of course they do', and wondered why that even mattered?

Years later, I visited France and I remember going into a bakery, smiling and pointing at what I wanted. I had no idea what the French words were for it. The shopkeeper smiled back and tried to help me out.

A smile really is the same in all languages – a happy, kind hello that tells the other person you are warm, welcoming and friendly.

It really is a language everyone shares.

How it works

A smile requires just thirteen muscles to work, whereas a frown takes 64 muscles; so it's actually EASIER to smile than to not!

Put a smile on each of the faces below, choosing which kind of smile to give to each character:

1 A big beamy smile

2 A tiny timid smile

3 A warm welcoming smile

4 A lots-of-teeth smile

5 An encouraging smile

6 A gentle smile

7 The biggest smile in the world, EVER!

8 A colourful smile

Then practise each of these smiles on a friend and have them guess which one you're doing – I bet they end up smiling too!

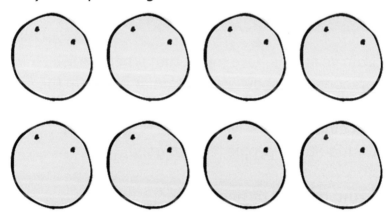

Create your own kindness...

...by sharing your lovely smile.

30. Everyone wins with kindness

Those who are happiest are those who do the most for others.
> - Booker T Washington
> (Educator, author and political advisor)

Did you know that feelings can be caught from others just like a cold?

That's why when we are in a bad mood, the people around us seem really grumpy. And it's why when we are in a great mood – all warm and smiley and jolly – the people around us seem that way too.

How it works

Brain scientists have found that when we see someone else show an emotion, it lights up the same areas of the brain as if we had experienced that emotion ourselves. So this is why being around happy people feels so good.

A 2010 Harvard Business School survey of happiness in 136 countries found that people who were generous were the happiest. So it's simple: hang out with happy people and be generous if you want to feel good. Everyone wins with kindness.

Haircut 100 (a very old pop band!)

My friend Johanna told me this great story about her children Sinéad, Senan and Aoife:

We were in the barber's at Christmas time, and an elderly gentleman was telling the barber he was having his hair cut for a very special party. He was turning 100, and his family were travelling from all over the world to attend it.

My three kids got whispering, and decided to pay for his haircut as a birthday gift for him. I was as chuffed as the man and his daughter were!

And the three kids who paid for the haircut? Full of happiness too.

Over to you

I always catch happiness when I give someone a present or bake someone a brilliant cake. What about you?

Can you think of a time you did something kind for someone and felt just as **FABULOUS** as they did?

Create your own kindness...

...by making someone (and yourself) feel amazing.

31. Pick up your pen

*We must find time to stop and thank the people
who make a difference in our lives.*
        - John F Kennedy (Former US president)

Writing is very powerful. In some ways it can have an even bigger impact than words because when something is written down it can be read again and again.

I have a letter from my mum that she wrote to me when I was leaving university. In it she tells me how proud she is of me and how she knows my life will be full of good things and how she loves me. She also thanked me for being her daughter.

How lovely is that?

I have read this letter hundreds of times and since my mum died it has brought me so much comfort.

The pen is powerful and it can communicate so much kindness.

How it works

Researchers at the University of Texas found that writing thank-you notes consistently put writers in a really good mood both before and after writing. They also found that the receivers of the notes appreciated them far more than the writers expected them to.

Everyone benefits!

Here are eight awesome ways to make someone smile through the written word:

1. You could write a note to your postie and pop it in the post box saying thanks for all the letters they deliver.

2. You could leave a comment on a vlog you have watched thanking the creator and telling them why you liked it.

3. You could leave a note on the kitchen table when you go to school saying 'Love you' to your family.

4. You could write a thank-you note to your teacher and leave it on their desk.

5. You could write a review online for a book you have read to tell the author how much you have enjoyed it and why (we really ♥ this).

6 Perhaps you could leave a sticky note on your bin thanking the refuse collector and wishing them a nice day.

7 After a drink in a café, you could leave a note saying thank you for your service next to your empty cup.

8 You could drop your granny a postcard saying 'cannot wait to see you next' or telling her your news.

Your notes don't have to be long or fancy or spelt right or perfect in any way. People just like to get a thank you or a hello. It warms their heart and lets them know they are appreciated and valued.

Activity: Write a thank-you note

Decide who you are going to write a note to and go ahead and do it. It can be far easier to write your thanks than say it and we know it is valued far more than you think it will be.

You can practise what you're going to say on the opposite page.

Create your own kindness...

...by sending a note of thanks into the world.

write your thank
you note here

32. Kindness to strangers

Remember there's no such thing as a small act of kindness. Every act creates a ripple with no logical end.

- Scott Adams (Comic strip creator)

Sometimes you will make a stranger so much happier just by a tiny act.

When we were in lockdown during the coronavirus pandemic, lots of people did small, kind things for strangers. Here are some I saw during that time:

- In the local park somebody had put fairy doors on the trees and created a magical forest.

- My daughter chalked a circle outside our house saying, 'Jump in and make a wish', and so many kids (and grown-ups too) were spotted doing this and beaming!

- Notes came through our door saying, 'if you need help with shopping just call', with the names of people we did not know.

It was so lovely to see how kind everyone was being to each other during the pandemic. It made everyone feel much better.

How it works

According to research from Emory University, when you are kind to someone else your brain's pleasure and reward centres light up just as they would if someone was kind to you.

This is called the 'helper's high' and it's an amazing feeling – like a little buzz of happiness. It's so good that you will want to be kind again and again so you keep on feeling it.

Activity: Your kindness story

I hope you are inspired by the wonderful stories of kindness to strangers below. What could your 'kindness to a stranger' story be?

Ruby made up writing sets of paper, envelopes, pens and stamps and gave them to a local care home.

Jamie and his mum made a free book box for their local community. They made a sign saying, 'please help yourself to books and please drop off any you have spare'.

Grace was walking down the road with her family when she saw a car hit the wing mirror of one of the vehicles parked on the road. It didn't stop. Grace checked it was clear and went out into the road to collect up all the pieces. She then went and knocked on the owner's door. The couple were so impressed at how helpful and honest she had been, one of them went back inside and brought her back a bar of chocolate.

write your
own kindness
to a stranger
story here

Create your own kindness...

FREE TO A
GOOD HOME!

...through your actions towards others.

A friend of mine once told me that every time she goes to the beach, she takes a bag with her to fill with rubbish before she leaves.

I have shared this story with lots of people and now every time I go to the beach I do it too. Perhaps now I've told you, you will take a bag with you to the beach and fill it with rubbish before you leave, and then maybe you will share this simple idea with someone else and they will do it too. (Do remember to wear protective gloves when you're picking up litter though!)

Each and every time we create a kindness story, no matter how tiny, we have the potential to make a huge difference by inspiring others to take action too.

The world may be HUGE but you are not too small to make a massive difference to it.

Are you ready to save the world, one act of kindness at a time?

Being kind to the world

33. Spread kind words across your community

Kind words can be short and easy to speak, but their echoes are truly endless.
- Mother Teresa (Nun and missionary)

We know kind words are powerful. Like Mother Teresa said in the quote above, they can be short and easy to speak but their impact lasts on and on.

How it works

In an experiment the same plants were placed in three separate rooms. In one room kind words were spoken, in the second cross words were spoken and in the third room no words were spoken.

Guess what happened?

Well the plants that were spoken to kindly grew a little bit more than the others. Words matter. If they affect plants this way, imagine how they can affect the people in your community. Maybe it makes them grow a little too.

Here are four simple ways to get kind words out into your community. Which one will you try first?

- Paint kind words on stones, then leave them around your neighbourhood to be found.

- Save some pocket money and take out an ad in a local newspaper that says *Kind people are the best kind of people*. If this is too expensive, how about writing it on a postcard and placing it in a shop window or noticeboard for a week?

- Chalk a message on the pavement or on a path to make someone smile. You could write something like 'Smile at the next person you see' or 'Wishing you a lovely day'.

- Make a poster for your window with an inspiring kindness quote on it so passers-by will see it. You could use one from this book?

DREAM

HOPE

IMAGINE

FRIEND

PEACE

Create your own kindness...

...by using and sharing kind words.

34. Noticing kindness

What we see depends mainly on what we look for.
— John Lubbock (Scientist and politician)

I don't know if you ever watch the news but it is often filled with stories that are about greed or poverty, illness or disaster or problems. Kindness isn't often featured on the news. It isn't considered important or interesting enough.

Generally, kindness doesn't get much attention until someone is unkind, then we give it lots of attention. However, the more attention we give to kindness, the bigger and more important it will become in all our lives.

GIVE SOMEONE YOU KNOW A HUG

MAKE SOMEONE LAUGH

TAKE SOME PET FOOD to A LOCAL SHELTER

donate to A charity

FEED the BIRDS

GIVE SOMEONE A COMPLIMENT

MAKE BREAKFAST FOR YOUR GROWN UP.

GIVE SOMEONE FLOWERS

MAKE SOMEONE A GIFT

ASK SOMEONE NEW to PLAY

HELP do THE CHORES

Did you know...?

Your brain has a filter that lets in the things you are focused on. This is called the reticular activating system (RAS). That's why you will always hear someone call your name even in a noisy room, or see someone wearing a yellow T-shirt if you are wearing a yellow T-shirt.

If you give lots of focus to kindness, you are telling your brain it is important. It will then automatically begin to notice more kindness and it will play a bigger part in your life.

Activity: Focus on kindness

Why not have a chat with your teacher at school and see if your class can produce a kindness newspaper full of stories and examples of kindness. Maybe you could include a kindness puzzle like the word search in this book, some great stories and examples of kindness?

Perhaps the newspaper could be made online to save paper, and emailed out to everyone's families too?

Create your own kindness...

...by giving kindness the attention it deserves!

35. World Kindness Day

Kindness is more important than wisdom, and the recognition of this is the beginning of wisdom.
        - Theodore Rubin (Psychiatrist and author)

By now we have come to see that kindness is much more important than being smart or wise. We have discovered that actually it's more important, more useful and more powerful than pretty much everything.

So kindness is most definitely worth celebrating.

World Kindness Day takes place on 13 November each year.

I think just like World Book Day, World Kindness Day should be celebrated in EVERY school.

If your school doesn't celebrate it, maybe this year YOU could encourage them to begin.

Did you know...?

World Kindness Day was started in 1998 by the World Kindness Movement, which is made up of kindness organizations from 28 different countries.

The aim of the World Kindness Movement and World Kindness Day is to 'create a kinder world by inspiring individuals and nations towards greater kindness'.

Isn't it lovely that across the world everyone is celebrating this VID (Very Important Day) with you?

Activity: Plan your World Kindness Day

On previous World Kindness Days, schools were asked to make colourful kites to chase grey clouds away and once, World Kindness UK gave away 10,000 chocolate bars at train stations – YUM!

What could World Kindness Day look like at your school?

Could there be bunting made, spelling out the word 'kindness'?

Could teachers read out stories of kindness?

Could there be a party filled with games and nice food to say hooray for kindness (a bit like a birthday party for kindness)?

What would be on your World Kindness Celebration plan? Let your imagination flow as you fill in your ideas on the opposite page.

You might want to share this plan with your teacher and see if any of your ideas could be put into action?

It's definitely a day to be celebrated.

Create your own kindness...

...by celebrating World Kindness Day.

36. Reverse advent calendar

We make a living by what we get. We make a life by what we give.

- Winston S. Churchill (Politician)

I am sure many of you have an advent calendar in the run-up to Christmas. It's exciting and leads up to the big day where you will hopefully eat well and get some great treats.

Not everyone is that fortunate though and lots of families struggle to afford things at Christmas time. You can help those families by having a reverse advent calendar.

What is it?

With a regular advent calendar, you open a window each day to see a picture or get a chocolate. With a reverse advent calendar, each day you simply add an item to a box which you then donate to your local food bank in time for Christmas.

It's all about the giving rather than the getting.

Even if you don't celebrate Christmas this is a really kind thing to do.

Did you know...?

Winter and Christmas are especially hard on people who are homeless or who live with poverty. Food banks help them get by with food donations. In December food banks get an increase of around 45 per cent in numbers of people needing support. More than 90 per cent of the food given out by food banks is donated by people like you.

It's best to start your reverse advent calendar in November so you can donate it to your local food bank in plenty of time for it to be given out for Christmas.

What to put in your box

It is worth finding out what your food bank wants by giving them a call or looking at their website. You can find your local food bank here and you will also find the address to drop items off at:

https://www.trusselltrust.org/get-help/find-a-foodbank/

They are usually after items that don't go off quickly:

- Rice
- Healthy snacks, such as dried fruit, nuts, crackers and oatcakes
- UHT milk
- Tea

- Coffee
- Jams
- Tinned soup
- Tinned beans
- Pasta

And toiletries like:

- Toothpaste
- Toilet paper
- Shower gel

- Shampoo
- Shaving cream

How to get your food bank items

You could use your pocket money to buy them or raid your cupboards at home (with permission!) to find things to donate. If you have no saved pocket money is there any way you could earn some? Perhaps you could encourage your wider family or neighbours, to donate to your box?

Activity: Make a reverse advent calendar

You will need:

- A box
- A little pocket money
- A list of items your food bank wants

A cardboard box is perfect for collecting items for your local food bank. Why not drop a handmade card inside your box, thanking the food bank volunteers for all their help?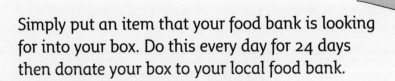

Simply put an item that your food bank is looking for into your box. Do this every day for 24 days then donate your box to your local food bank.

Create your own kindness...

...by giving what you can this Christmas.

37. Bee kind

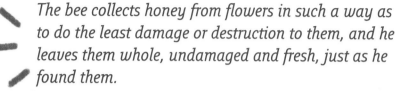

The bee collects honey from flowers in such a way as to do the least damage or destruction to them, and he leaves them whole, undamaged and fresh, just as he found them.

- Saint Francis de Sales

Apart from people, bees are the most studied creature in the whole world, and rightly so. They are amazing and they are important, as they do such a vital job of helping to pollinate plants.

Did you know...?

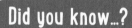

Bees save UK farmers 1.8 billion pounds a year by pollinating farms for free and helping their crops grow. Bees actually play a key role in one of every three bites we eat.

In Europe, 1 in 10 wild bees are about to become extinct. Climate change, drought and floods all make life harder for bees. With so many chemicals being used in farming, and so much countryside being built on, it all adds to the plight of the bee.

They need our help.

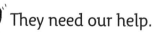

BZZ

Activity: Save our bees

Here are three ways you can help bees to survive:

1 **Give them food**

Bees love these fruits, flowers and plants, so planting more of them can really make a difference:

- Lavender
- Apple trees (you only need to save a pip from your apple!)
- Ivy
- Crocus
- Snowdrops
- Strawberries
- Wildflowers like poppies, cornflowers and cowslips
- Primrose
- Marigolds
- Buddleia

Bees like herbs too. Maybe you could plant a little herb garden?

Bees especially like:

- Chives
- Sage
- Rosemary
- Thyme
- Marjoram

You don't need to have a big garden in order to grow any of these and they can all be started in pots.

If you don't have anywhere to grow these plants, why not suggest to your teacher a little bee-friendly project for your class involving a bit of research and some planting?

Be sure to research the plants you want to grow first so that you plant them in the right season and you know how to look after them.

2 Give them a drink

Just like us, bees need water to survive. They especially like rainwater.

You could fill a small bucket or tray with rainwater, and put a few stones in it that are large and stable enough to give bees a safe place to drink from.

You could also float old wine corks in your bucket, anything that gives bees something to land on so they can have their drink.

3 Give them first aid

If you see a bee that looks like it's dying, it may just need a little energy boost. Mix equal volumes of sugar and water to make sugar water and place a teaspoon or bottle lid of it right next to the bee. You might just save its life.

Create your own kindness...

...by being a friend to the bees.

38. Picking up litter

Be part of the solution, not the pollution!
                    - Environmental Action slogan

Litter is a big problem.

It is dangerous to wildlife and it is ugly, smelly and unpleasant.

Picking up litter is an excellent way to show your community some kindness. It doesn't look its best when covered in rubbish does it?

Did you know...?

The world spends over 8 billion pounds a year cleaning up litter – just think how many people that money could help!

According to the CPRE (Campaign to Protect Rural England), the three major problems are fast-food packaging, sweet wrappers and drinks bottles made from plastic, tin or glass.

What can you do to help?

If you take a look at the Keep Britain Tidy website you can sign yourself up to become a #LitterHero and take part in The Great British Spring Clean, a yearly campaign with a simple aim: to bring people across the country together to clear up rubbish.

You don't have to wait for a special day though, you can join local groups or even organize your own litter pick:

- Do contact your local council. Lots of them are really happy to support litter picks by providing equipment, black bags and high visibility vests. They can sometimes collect the bags of litter at the end of your event too.

- Send out invites giving a time and place to meet, ensuring people bring bin liners for rubbish and gloves for hygiene and to protect hands, plus a bottle of water to keep themselves hydrated.

- Get litter picking!

Create your own kindness...

...by becoming a litter hero.

39. A solution for loneliness

We can change the world and make it a better place. It is in our hands to make a difference.
- Nelson Mandela (Anti-apartheid revolutionary and former President of South Africa)

A recent study, by the British Red Cross found over one million older people often or always feel lonely.

I have a friend called Lyndsey Young who decided to do something about it. She created The Friendly Bench™ – safe, easily accessible community gardens with seating for people to come together.

Providing a place for lonely people to gather and make new friends was a brilliant solution!

How it works

Scientists have discovered that loneliness can be as bad for someone's health as smoking!

Lyndsey decided to do something about loneliness. She thought hard, worked hard, got lots of support and in the end she created a brilliant solution to loneliness. Now it's over to you.

Activity: Find a loneliness solution

Have a go at inventing a solution to the problem of loneliness for either older people in your community or perhaps kids at your school:

1. Define your problem and write it clearly in the centre of a piece of paper.
2. Mind map lots of ideas for solving the problem.
3. Pick one of your solutions and write down 5 steps to achieving it.
4. Make a list of people who might be able to help you put it into action.

If your idea doesn't work why not try another of your ideas. An inventor never fails; they are just practising till they get it right.

Create your own kindness...

...by tackling loneliness step by step.

131

40. The great kindness bake off

Being kind is a piece of cake.

- Author unknown

Baking someone a treat is a great way to show kindness and one of my favourite things to do for a friend who may be feeling a bit down.

You could bake for your family, your class, a friend, a local care home or for a bake sale to raise money for charity.

Wherever possible do check to see if people have specific diets, such as gluten free, vegan or dairy free, so you can try and meet their needs.

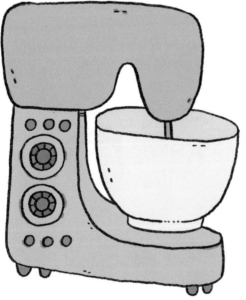

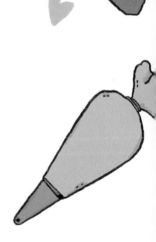

How it works

Scientists have found that doing little creative acts (like baking) help people feel more relaxed and happier.

They believe this is because baking is an act of mindfulness. Being mindful means being present, focusing on the detail of what you're doing and not worrying about other things. This gives your mind a rest and lets it relax.

Happiness comes because you have something lovely at the end of it — either to eat or to give to others.

Activity: Cook up some kindness

Easy vegan scones
Makes 6–8 scones
- 225g self-raising flour
- 50g vegan butter
- pinch of salt
- 25g caster sugar
- 50g sultanas or other dried fruit (optional)
- 125ml almond milk

1. Preheat the oven to 220°C / gas mark 7. Grease a baking tray.

2. Put the flour and salt in a mixing bowl. Add the butter and, using your fingers, rub the mixture together until it looks like breadcrumbs.

3. Stir in the sugar, add the optional dried fruit, and mix well.

4. Add milk and stir to bind it all together, then knead the mixture until you have a firm dough.

5. Roll out the dough until it is about 2cm thick.

6. Cut out shapes with a round cookie cutter or the rim of a small cup.

7. Put the vegan scones on a baking tray, brush them with almond milk and cook for about 15 minutes (but keep checking!) until they are golden on top.

Coconut ice squares

- 200g desiccated coconut
- 250g icing sugar
- 250g tin of sweet condensed milk
- A few drops of food colouring

1. Pour the condensed milk into a big bowl and mix in the coconut and icing sugar really well.

2. Split your mixture into two.

3. Add a few drops of food colouring to one half of the mixture and mix it in well.

4. Sprinkle icing sugar on your work surface and get a rolling pin.

5. Roll each half out into rectangles of about the same size and 1.5 cm thick.

6. Put them on top of each other, squashing them down slightly so they stick together.

7. Lift it up with a fish slice and put on to a tray lined with baking paper.

8. Put in a cool place overnight to set.

9. Cut the coconut ice into about 8 small square pieces and store them in an airtight container, where they will keep for up to 4 weeks.

Create your own kindness...

...by getting your bake on.

41. Beautiful brilliant butterflies

'Just living is not enough,' said the butterfly, 'one must have sunshine, freedom and a little flower.'
- Hans Christian Anderson (storyteller)

There are 59 types of butterfly species in Britain, and another 30 species come here to visit from other parts of Europe. How many can you name?

Did you know...?

Numbers of butterflies have decreased over recent years due to pollution, changing weather patterns and more of the countryside being built on. The good news, though, is that even people with tiny gardens can actually provide them with a lot of what they need.

There are three ways you can help butterflies:

1. Leave out ripe fruit for them such as over-ripe pears, plums and apples.

2. Don't use chemical sprays on plants that are flowering.

3. Plant colourful flowers that they love, such as bluebells, lavender, cornflowers, primroses and buddleia.

Activity: Make a butterfly feeder

You will need:
- a sponge
- 1 cup of water
- 3 teaspoons of sugar
- string

1. Boil the kettle and pour out a cup of water (ask an adult to help).

2. Stir in 3 teaspoons of sugar until dissolved and leave to cool.

3. Cut your sponge into small pieces and poke a hole in each one.

4. Cut a 10cm piece of string and push it through the hole in the sponge.

5. Dip the sponge in the syrup and let it soak it up.

6. Hang it somewhere shady, near flowers if possible, so the butterflies can have a drink.

Create your own kindness...

...by taking care of nature and all her creatures whenever and wherever you can.

42. Gifts of nature

Your acts of kindness ... linger and continue to uplift others long after your sharing.

— Rumi (Persian poet)

I love surprises, don't you?

If I find a stone tower on the beach or a whirl of arranged shells it makes me smile. I have no idea who created these little bits of art in nature but I feel that someone somewhere just gave me a little gift.

Did you know...?

Mandala is a Sanskrit term that means 'circle'. A mandala is a circular shape with a design that spans out symmetrically from the centre. Buddhists believe they represent the universe, and that creating a mandala or looking at one is supposed to help you feel more balanced.

Pattern making is very good for your mind, which makes this a great way to deal with any stress or anxiety you feel.

Activity: Make a nature mandala

A mandala made from nature can be as simple or as complicated as you like. You can use any fallen or found items, such as:

- Pebbles
- Stones
- Grass
- Fallen flowers
- Sticks
- Acorns
- Pine cones
- Leaves
- Conkers

1. Start with a large central object and work your way outwards – you might want to use a hula hoop or chalk a circle to help contain your design.

2. Create a circle around your centre item.

3. Add layer after layer until you are happy with your design.

4. Take a photo of your creation.

5. Leave it to be found and imagine all the people who will smile at it.

Create your own kindness...

...by making someone smile with nature art.

43. Eco Bingo

In a world of more than seven billion people, each of us is a drop in the bucket. But with enough drops, we can fill any bucket.

- David Suzuki (Environmental activist and scientist)

You don't pay the bills in your house or decide who supplies your electricity. Maybe you think that the amount of energy used in your home is up to the adults who live there.

Of course it is largely up to adults in your house to make smart decisions about energy use, but not completely. There are many things you can do to make a difference to the world, beginning with your actions at home.

Did you know…?

Every time we use energy that comes from fossil fuels (like petrol and electricity), we create a gas called carbon dioxide (CO_2).

When there is too much of CO_2 in the Earth's atmosphere, heat gets trapped, causing temperatures to rise and climate change to occur, which damages our planet.

The amount of CO_2 we release from our actions is called our **carbon footprint** and we need to try and make our individual footprint as small as we can.

A lot of CO_2 is made in houses (almost 30 per cent) so there is a lot you can do to make a difference by changing what you do in your home.

Activity: Reduce your carbon footprint

If you have ever done book bingo at school you will know just what to do with this Eco Bingo card. You simply cross out each activity as you try one, until you have done them all.

When you have completed your bingo card yell 'Eco Bingo!' really loudly then fill in the certificate below. Be proud, knowing you have started up some good habits that really will make a difference.

Fill in the certificate when you have completed your bingo card.

I _____

have completed my Eco Bingo challenge and have taken important steps towards reducing my carbon footprint.

Have a shower instead of a bath.	Turn off the light as you leave the room.	Donate 3 items of clothing that no longer fit to a charity shop.
Turn off the water while you're brushing your teeth.	Use things from your recycling bin for a craft project.	Have a meatless Monday.
Learn a great leftovers recipe.	Walk somewhere you would usually drive to.	Wear the same outfit twice to save laundry.
Don't leave electrical items on standby.	Gift a board game you no longer play to another family.	Mend something that is broken.

Create your own kindness...

...by doing your bit to save the planet.

44. A homemade craft box

No act of kindness, no matter how small, is ever wasted.

- Aesop (Ancient Greek storyteller)

Landfill is the name used for the areas where all of our un-recycled, unwanted items go. Harmful gases and chemicals are released from the rubbish in landfill sites, causing pollution.

How it works

When the contents of your recycling bin are collected, they get broken down and re-made into something new. But even recycling takes up energy, in transporting the object, breaking it down and creating a new object. Reusing is even better.

Reusing what you have is a brilliant way of being kind to the planet and everyone who lives upon it. Once it becomes a habit you will do it without even really thinking.

It has also been found that people who care about the environment are happier.

Activity: Create a homemade craft box

A homemade craft box can be filled with all sorts of things that you might otherwise throw away. You just need to use your imagination.

For everything you might possibly want to reuse, you will find tutorials on YouTube showing you how.

In it could go:

- Ribbon
- Wooden pegs
- Small pieces of cut-up fabric
- Wool
- Pasta shells
- Bubble wrap

- Old magazines
- Old birthday cards
- Small squares of aluminium foil
- Cotton wool
- An old shirt for painting

What are you going to make from your homemade craft box?

Create your own kindness...

...by reusing items you already have to help take the pressure off our planet.

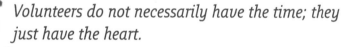

45. The value in volunteering

Volunteers do not necessarily have the time; they just have the heart.

> - Elizabeth Andrew (Welsh suffragette and political activist)

When you volunteer, you give your time for free to support a cause or help out in some way. Volunteering is a brilliant way to learn new skills, make new friends and help out a cause you care about.

You could volunteer to:

- Help at a stall at your school's Christmas Fair
- Help your Grandad to tidy his garden
- Stay behind after football practice and collect the cones
- Help to teach a younger child to read
- Bring the class pet home to look after in the holidays (ask your grown-up first!)
- Help at an animal rescue centre
- Sort items at your local charity shop
- Bag items at the supermarket for charity
- Sing with the school choir at a care home

How it works

By now you will know that doing kind things for other people is a quick route to being happy yourself, so of course volunteering will make you feel good.

But did you know that volunteering makes people healthier too. One research study of over 7,000 people found that 40 per cent of volunteers spend less time in hospital.

Volunteering is also believed to reduce stress as it's hard to feel tense when you are focusing on something other than yourself.

Activity: Get involved

Have a think about something you could volunteer to do. Maybe you could get a friend or your family involved if you feel a little shy.

- What's your idea?
- What do you need to do to make it happen?
- Who can help you?

Create your own kindness...

...by giving your time to help in different ways throughout your life.

46. All the fun of fundraising

We rise by lifting others.

- Maya Angelou (Author and activist)

Fundraising is when you raise money for a cause or charity through your efforts.

As a kid you might feel quite powerless when it comes to helping people or causes because you don't have much money. But fundraising can make you feel empoweredand help you to make a difference.

There are so many ways to fundraise, from car boot sales to karaoke nights, putting on a talent show to a sponsored silence.

How it works

Never feel bad about raising money – you are making people happy. Researchers have found that givers are more happy than non-givers.

In fact, they're 43 per cent more likely than non-givers to say they are 'very happy'. And you asking for a donation is part of that!

Activity: Five steps to fundraising success

1. Think about which cause to raise money for.
2. Rope in some helpers (unless you plan to do it solo).
3. Make a mind map of ideas on how to fundraise.
4. Settle on the idea you like best (and which is most do-able).
5. Put it into action.

colour me

Donations

What not to do

There are some things you can't do if you are under 13:

- Street and house-to-house collections.
- Lotteries or raffles.
- Events involving alcohol.

But don't worry about that because there are many, many other things you can do instead!

What fundraising teaches you

The cause you are raising money for isn't the only thing to benefit from your fundraising. It teaches you money skills, how to think creatively, empathise with others in need, and to feel part of a community that cares. It can also be loads of fun to fundraise!

Some fabulous fundraisers

- When she was 10, my daughter Lise and her friend made a magazine full of puzzles and how-tos and sold it (along with doing a book and cake sale) to raise £100 for Rainbows Hospice.

- Tom lives in Tasmania and is 11. He does a toy and book clear-out every year and sells them to raise money for Sea Shepherd, which is a marine conservation organization. He usually raises about $100 a year.

- Izzy lives in Nottingham and raised money for the Little Princess Trust when she was 9. She spent nearly 2 years growing her hair so she could cut it and send it to the charity. She also managed to raise £500 in sponsorship. She was aiming for £500 as that's the full cost of making and fitting a custom wig for a child.

- Ben is from Manchester. He raised £650 for Diabetes UK by taking part in the Ride Yorkshire Sportive and cycling 40 miles just two weeks after his 10th birthday.

- Amelie is 8 and Lottie is 5 and they live in Yateley, Hampshire. They raised £500 for the NHS fund by making and selling rainbow loom bracelets.

- Pip and Max raised £40 for the RSPCA when they were 6 and 8. They made cupcakes and sold them to their neighbours.

- Alexander aged 10 from Nottinghamshire is also raising money for the NHS by doing a 200-mile bike ride. At the time of writing he has raised £535.

Amazing! Huge well done to all these superstars – what fabulous fundraising ideas they put into action.

Create your own kindness...

...by fundraising for a cause you believe in.

47. Random acts of kindness

How do we change the world? One random act of kindness at a time.

- Morgan Freeman (Actor)

A random act of kindness is when you do something kind for someone unexpectedly and for no other reason than to be kind.

How it works

Scientists have found that when we do a good deed for others, our brains release a 'feel-good' hormone called oxytocin – sometimes called the love hormone. Other feel-good chemicals are also released including dopamine (which gives us a feeling of euphoria) and serotonin (which boosts our mood).

A random act of kindness is a wonderful thing to do. Which of these will you try first?

Create your own kindness...

...by doing random acts of kindness and making someone's day.

Gift your week's pocket money to charity.

Make up a parcel for a homeless person.

Donate old toys to a charity shop.

Plant something.

Bake for your grandparents.

Tidy your room without being asked.

Feed the ducks (seed, not bread).

Smile at a passer-by.

Let someone go in front of you in a queue.

Give someone an unexpected compliment.

Write a thank you note to someone who teaches you.

Make a get-well card for someone.

Make a bookmark and leave it in a library book.

Help to make dinner.

Offer to help your teacher tidy up at break.

Give someone (you know) a big hug.

48. Create a kindness board game

Playing games can be so much fun and games can actually really make you think.

When I play Monopoly I think about building up a whole street of houses and making lots of money.

When I play Scrabble I want to learn every word in the dictionary so I can't be defeated again.

When I play Cluedo I often think I'd like to be a detective and when I lose (always) at Mario Kart I dream about being a racing driver.

Whatever we focus on grows bigger and bigger in our mind. So a kindness board game is a wonderful thing to play as it can help you become even kinder.

How it works

Playing board games is a great way to spend time with your family and friends, but there are many more benefits to taking part than just passing the time.

Did you know that playing board games is like a workout for the brain?

Our brain is like a muscle and needs exercising in order to work really well. Researchers found that playing board games a couple of times a week can increase brain speed by around 30 per cent!

Even more amazing than that, they can improve your memory, develop your ability to solve problems and boost your immune system.

Laughing and spending quality time with loved ones also releases endorphins (the chemicals in our bodies that increase happiness).

Activity: Create your own game

I've invented my own version of a kindness Snakes and Ladders on the next page, and I'd love for you to give it a go!

Every time you land on a square that has a kind act, you can move up. Beware the unkind actions, though, as those will make you slip back down the board.

Can you create a kindness board game of your own? Maybe a version of Ludo or Dominoes or something entirely original.

This can be a great activity to try with friends or family members, and it's a fantastic way of boosting your creativity. Plus, you get all the benefits of playing games that we mentioned on the previous page.

Ready? Go!

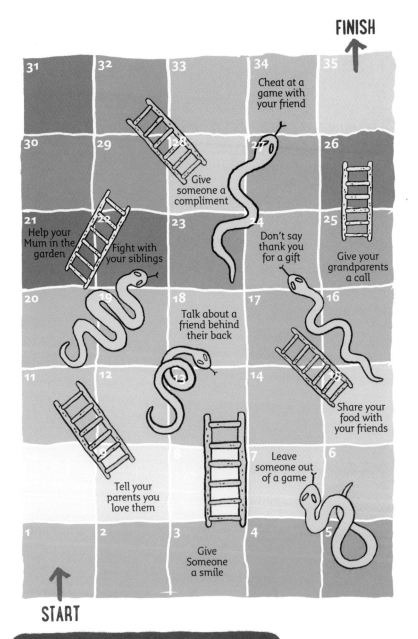

49. Shout about it

Each time a man stands up for an ideal, or acts to improve the lot of others, or strikes out against injustice, he sends forth a tiny ripple of hope.

— Robert F Kennedy (Politician and lawyer)

As a child, what can you do about something that bothers you in your community or in the environment? Do you feel that because you are small, no one will listen to what you have to say?

You are way more powerful than you realize and you do have a voice. You just need to make it heard.

So what can you do?

You could make a poster for your window.

You could write to a newspaper like *First News* or *The Week Junior* and speak up about your cause.

You could speak in front of your class or maybe even in front of your school at an assembly.

Perhaps you could write to your MP.

Activity: How to write to your MP

Anyone in the UK can contact their local MP about any issues or causes they feel strongly about. You can contact them by phone, email, letter or you can even have a meeting with them. Don't be shy. They work for you.

If they agree to support a cause you have raised with them, they may also choose to raise it in the House of Commons and even the prime minister might get to hear about it.

You can find out who your local MP is here
https://members.parliament.uk/members/Commons

What might your letter say?

Create your own kindness...

...by speaking up about the causes you believe will make life better.

50. Your kindness journey

Everywhere you go, leave a glitter trail of kindness behind you.

- Author unknown

Throughout this book you have learned the importance of being kind to yourself, to others and to the wider world.

Now it's time to go and put all that learning into action.

Life is a long journey and you're still pretty near the start. That means you have so many chances to make a difference to all the people and projects your life will touch.

What an opportunity you have to sprinkle kindness everywhere, what a difference you can make throughout the journey of your life.

Go forth and be kind!

THE AWARD FOR Kindness Goes to